Original title:
Icy Horizons

Copyright © 2024 Swan Charm
All rights reserved.

Author: Olivia Oja
ISBN HARDBACK: 978-9916-79-765-5
ISBN PAPERBACK: 978-9916-79-766-2
ISBN EBOOK: 978-9916-79-767-9

The Quiet Song of White-Washed Earth

In the stillness of dawn's light,
A whisper floats on gentle air.
White-washed hills stand bold and bright,
Nature's canvas, pure and fair.

Shadows dance where cold winds sweep,
Crystalline dreams in soft repose.
Beneath the snow, the secrets keep,
A world that quietly bestows.

Silence echoes, sweet and clear,
Footprints mark the pristine ground.
Each step taken, calm and near,
In the hush, true peace is found.

Branches bare, like fingers stretched,
Reach for skies of endless blue.
Each soft sigh, a heart enetched,
In the white-washed world, anew.

As twilight brings the stars to rise,
The quiet song begins to play.
In moonlit glow, our spirits fly,
Guided by the night's ballet.

Glistening Paths Through an Icy Wilderness

Frozen lakes reflect the sky,
A tapestry of diamond light.
Nature's mirror, high and nigh,
Guiding wanderers through the night.

Each footfall crackles underfoot,
A sound like whispers on the breeze.
In this land, the world is mute,
Time itself seems loath to tease.

Tall trees wear coats of crystal frost,
Branches laden, heavy with grace.
In this silence, nothing's lost,
Every moment finds its place.

Glistening paths, both wild and free,
Lead the heart to deeper dreams.
In the chill, we come to see,
Life's wonders glimmer in moonbeams.

As shadows stretch and daylight wanes,
The wilderness begins to sigh.
A fleeting warmth that gently reigns,
Calls us forth to say goodbye.

Hushed Landscapes

In fields where silence blooms,
Beneath the gentle sky,
Shadows of the twilight loom,
As whispers softly sigh.

The trees stand straight and tall,
Draped in twilight's grace,
While dusk begins to call,
The stars find their place.

A brook flows, calm and slow,
Reflecting fading light,
Where dreams and shadows go,
Into the tranquil night.

Mountains wear a silver crown,
Wrapped in misty veils,
Nature wears a sleepy gown,
As night begins her tales.

In the heart of the still,
The world breathes a sigh,
Wrapped in time's soft thrill,
Beneath the endless sky.

Frost-kissed Awakening

Morning breaks with soft embrace,
The frost blankets the ground.
Nature's breath, a whispered grace,
Where peace and chill are found.

Sunrise paints the icy trees,
With hues of gold and blush,
As gentle winds begin to tease,
The silence breaks, a hush.

Footprints trace through fields of white,
A journey starts anew,
Each step reveals pure, soft light,
In every glistened view.

Birds chirp their dawn delight,
Amidst a sparkling glow,
As day dispels the night,
Revealing all below.

With every breath, the world awakes,
To warmth the sun will bring,
In frost-kissed lands, the heart breaks,
And finds its song to sing.

Boundless Winter

Underneath the endless sky,
Snowflakes dance and weave,
A soft and silent lullaby,
In winter's breath, we believe.

Mountains stretch with arms so wide,
Wrapped in a frosty quilt,
Where secrets of the night reside,
In every flake that's spilt.

Fields glisten like a diamond sea,
As twilight meets the day,
A boundless realm, wild and free,
Where shadows softly play.

A memory of warmth once shared,
Echoes through the cold,
In this realm, our hearts are bared,
With stories yet untold.

In winter's chill, life holds its breath,
Awaiting spring's embrace,
Through the dance of life and death,
Time moves with gentle grace.

Clear-Cut Chill

In the forest's quiet shade,
Whispers of the cold,
Blades of grass, a frosted braid,
In a tale retold.

Icicles hang like crystal spears,
From branches bent and bare,
Each layer holds the weight of years,
In the cool, crisp air.

A lonely path through snowy glade,
Leads where silence reigns,
With every step, the world has made,
A beauty free from chains.

The sky wears a cloak of gray,
A shroud of winter's might,
Yet in the stillness of the day,
There's magic in the light.

As daylight fades, the chill descends,
Embracing all around,
In the clear-cut winter bends,
A symphony of sound.

Whitewashed Memories

Faded photographs on the wall,
Whispers of laughter, echoes call.
Dusty corners hold their grace,
Time unravels, leaves no trace.

Moments frozen, lost in time,
Sweet serenity in the climb.
Memories wrapped in soft embrace,
An old album's worn-out face.

Days of youth, bright and free,
Chasing shadows, you and me.
Every smile, a fragile thread,
Stitched together, love unbled.

Though the seasons may depart,
These whitewashed dreams fill the heart.
Through the years, they gently roam,
In each chamber, they find home.

Arctic Embrace

Cold winds whisper secrets clear,
In the stillness, echoes near.
Blanket of snow, pure and white,
Stars above, a guiding light.

Reflections dance on icy lakes,
Nature's beauty, breath it takes.
Frozen pines, a silent prayer,
In this moment, we find care.

Hand in hand, through winter's breath,
Finding warmth, defying death.
Embers glow in frigid night,
Hearts entwined, two souls ignite.

The Arctic holds its breath for us,
In this beauty, we find trust.
Through the frost, we will embrace,
Love eternal, in this space.

Frigid Horizons

Beyond the valleys, ice unfolds,
In the silence, bravery holds.
Chasing dreams on crystal fields,
Every heartbeat, freedom yields.

Mountains rise to touch the sky,
Hope takes flight, let spirits fly.
Blizzards rage with fierce intent,
Yet warmth within us, heaven-sent.

Colors fade in winter's grasp,
Nature's breath, a gentle rasp.
Footprints left on silver trails,
Tales of love where courage sails.

In the distance, horizons call,
We seek the paths that rise and fall.
Frigid air, a reminder sweet,
Every journey makes us complete.

Numbed Serenity

In the hush of falling snow,
Time stands still, the world aglow.
Peace enfolds like a gentle shawl,
Wrapped in silence, we hear the call.

Fingers trace the ice-cold glass,
Memories linger, moments pass.
Numbed from pain, we find our way,
Serenity blooms in shades of gray.

Hearts that ache beneath the frost,
Find solace in the love we've lost.
Nature whispers, soft and kind,
Healing solace, intertwined.

Each breath clear in the wintry mist,
Holding tight to joy and bliss.
Through the stillness, we reclaim,
Numbed serenity, life's sweet game.

Glacial Thoughts Under Winter Skies

Cold winds whisper softly,
Carrying secrets untold.
Mountains wear their white blanket,
As the night unfolds.

Stars twinkle like dreams,
High above in the deep.
Silent hopes drift slowly,
While the world lays asleep.

Each breath is a fog,
Dance of the frigid air.
Nature holds its stillness,
With a beauty so rare.

A crystal-clear pond,
Mirrors the vast night.
Thoughts drift like snowflakes,
In a world bathed in white.

Underneath the moon,
Whispers the icy ground.
Heartbeats sync with silence,
In this frozen surround.

Shadows of Silence in the Frosted Expanse

Moonlight casts a spell,
On the frosted trees.
Branches bend and sway,
In the soft, cold breeze.

Echoes of the night,
Wrapped in gentle hush.
Pale shadows gather,
In the quiet rush.

Blankets of white stretch,
Over hills and fields.
Time stands still within,
Nature's quiet yields.

Footprints in the snow,
Stories left behind.
Whispers of the past,
In the chill we find.

Stars above us shimmer,
In the expansive dome.
Silence speaks in volumes,
In this vast, cold home.

Frozen Reflections Under a Starlit Veil

The lake lies as a mirror,
Beneath the starry sky.
Dreams float like feathers,
As moments drift by.

Ripples tell the tale,
Of a night crystal clear.
Frozen worlds awaken,
To the sounds we hold dear.

A blanket of starlight,
Cascades softly down.
Each beam a reminder,
Of beauty in the brown.

In the stillness of night,
Thoughts glide like a swan.
Reflections of our hearts,
In the dawn's early yawn.

Whispers in the silence,
In the cold air's embrace.
These frozen reflections,
Time cannot erase.

The Dance of Frost Upon the Horizon's Edge

Frost paints every surface,
In delicate flair.
A ballet on the rooftops,
In the wintry air.

Sunrise kisses lightly,
Chasing shadows away.
The dance of frost begins,
To welcome the day.

Nature's silent rhythm,
Plays upon the ground.
In the quiet morning,
A new world is found.

Each crystal a story,
Whispers of the cold.
As warmth begins to linger,
And the sun takes hold.

On the horizon's edge,
Beauty unfolds wide.
The dance of frost and light,
In the winter's stride.

Treading Lightly on Glassy Plains

The morning dew, a soft embrace,
Each step we take, a careful trace.
The horizon gleams with whispered light,
As dreams emerge from gentle night.

With every breath, the silence sings,
Awakening the world as spring brings.
The crystal grass beneath our feet,
A tender dance, so pure, so sweet.

In open air, our joys collide,
As shadows play, and hopes abide.
We wander wide, no end in sight,
On glassy plains, our hearts take flight.

Beneath the sky, so vast, so blue,
We feel the earth, each pulse, each hue.
Treading softly, with grace bestowed,
We carve a path on this soft road.

And in the stillness, moments freeze,
The fleeting time, a gentle tease.
Together here, on nature's stage,
We write our tale, page by page.

Horizons Bound in Crystal Virginity

From peaks so high, the world unfolds,
A canvas pure, where truth beholds.
Horizons stretch, a soft refrain,
In crystal dreams, our souls remain.

The mountains crown the skies so deep,
Where silent winds collect and sweep.
Each sunbeam dances, bright and bold,
A story whispered, yet untold.

The air is crisp, with joy it binds,
As nature gently redefines.
With every glance, we venture near,
To worlds untouched, serene and clear.

In hidden nooks, the secrets lie,
Where time stands still, and spirits fly.
We chase the dusk, our hearts akin,
In crystal realms, our lives begin.

A symphony of light and peace,
In every breath, we find release.
With every pulse, the earth we greet,
In boundless love, we are complete.

The Chill of Distant Glimmers

At twilight's edge, the chill descends,
As fading light begins to bend.
From distant shores, the glimmers call,
A beckoning to us, one and all.

The stars awake, in silence bloom,
Illuminating the creeping gloom.
With gentle whispers, night reveals,
The secrets hidden, time conceals.

Each breath of wind, a ghostly sigh,
As shadows dance beneath the sky.
In moonlight's glow, our visions twine,
A tapestry of dreams divine.

Through haunted woods, we weave our fate,
Embracing moments, never late.
The chill reminds us of our place,
In cosmic realms, we find our grace.

From distant glimmers, hope ignites,
Awakening the darkest nights.
With every flicker, courage grows,
In chill's embrace, our spirit flows.

Vast White Silhouettes in the Twilight

In twilight's glow, the silence reigns,
As shadows stretch across the plains.
The world adorned in shades of white,
With silhouettes that fade from sight.

The snowflakes fall, a whispered dance,
Each flake a dream, a fleeting chance.
We wander through this quiet land,
In winter's grasp, we take a stand.

With every step, the echoes sing,
Of stories told by winter's wing.
The frosty air, a breath of peace,
In vastness found, our hearts release.

Beneath the stars, a blanket wide,
In twinkling light, our hopes abide.
The night entwines, so soft, so still,
In white silhouettes, we find our will.

Together here, in tender grace,
We trace the contours of this space.
In twilight's arms, forever bright,
We dream our dreams in silver light.

Specter of Snow

Whispers fall like feathers, soft,
A blanket wraps the weary ground.
Ghostly figures drift aloft,
In twilight's hush, their dance renowned.

Silent woods, a shimmering white,
Footprints vanish, as if in dreams.
Moonlit beams on the frozen night,
Each shadow knows what silence screams.

Wisps of breath in the chilly air,
Dancing flakes weave tales untold.
Crystals hanging without a care,
In this realm, the heart feels bold.

Echoes linger, a distant tune,
Stories spun in the winter's light.
By the cold glow of a fading moon,
The specter glides, taking flight.

Time is paused, a captive here,
In the marvel of the snowy cloak.
Laughter fades, replaced by fear,
As night devours the dawn's soft stroke.

Enchanted Icefield

Amidst the frost, a world unfolds,
Where dreams and whispers interlace.
Every crystal a story holds,
In the cold, we find our place.

Glistening waves of frozen seas,
Echoes dance on the frosty breeze.
Time stands still as magic swells,
In the heart of these icy dells.

Beneath the stars, a canvas white,
A tapestry of pure delight.
Fires gleam in the cool expanse,
With every snowflake, we take a chance.

A realm where fantasies take flight,
In shadows kissed by candle glow.
Hearts alight with pure delight,
In the magic of the icefield's flow.

Legends painted in each deep breath,
Life entwined with dreams cascading.
In this sphere of ice and death,
The heart finds love, never fading.

Shattered Silence

In the pause of snow's soft fall,
Whispers rustle, yet none can hear.
Nature's breath, a silent call,
Layers thick, concealing fear.

Cracks in the quiet, sharp and fierce,
Memories buried 'neath a veil.
Echoes of voices that still pierce,
Through the frost, a haunting tale.

Footsteps crunch on the frozen ground,
Eyes search for what once was here.
In broken stillness, shadows abound,
Each glance holds both hope and fear.

Hearts beat slow, in the wintry chill,
As time cascades in still despair.
Yet in the void, a flicker, a thrill,
Glimmers of warmth linger in air.

From quiet depths, new voices rise,
Cracks in silence, love takes its stand.
In winter's clasp, where truth defies,
Emerges warmth, a guiding hand.

Beyond the Frost

Underneath a frozen sky,
Where whispers linger, hopes abide.
Silent dreams, we wonder why,
The world grows still, time's cruel tide.

In shadows cast by moonlit beams,
A flicker sparks within the heart.
Beyond the frost, we chase our dreams,
As dawn unfolds, new journeys start.

Beneath the layers, warmth awaits,
A fiery glow in winter's depth.
We brave the chill, defy our fates,
In every breath, the world's adept.

Glowing embers, hidden bright,
Nature's fury, tender grace.
Through icy grips, we see the light,
A chance to dry the frost's embrace.

So step with faith, tread carefully,
Each heart a beacon, bold and free.
For in the frost, we find the key,
To realms of hope, eternally.

Glinting Snowflakes

Softly they dance upon the air,
Whispers of winter, beyond compare.
Crystal jewels on the ground below,
Each a story, each a glow.

Fleeting moments, a quiet grace,
Embraced in silence, a soft embrace.
They sparkle bright in the morning light,
Transforming the world, pure and white.

Falling gently, a tender kiss,
A fleeting beauty, a snowy bliss.
They melt away, yet memories stay,
In every heart, they find a way.

Under the sun, they shimmer and shine,
Little wonders, oh how they twine.
Nature's magic, a wondrous sight,
Glinting snowflakes, pure delight.

Ember of dreams in the winter's clutch,
Each unique, each a gentle touch.
As they fall, the world stands still,
In awe of nature, we feel the thrill.

Silent Glaciers

Majestic giants, still and cold,
Secrets of ages, tales untold.
Crystal blue, they silently gleam,
A frozen fortress, a timeless dream.

Carving valleys with a gentle might,
Whispers of wisdom in the night.
They calve along the icy edge,
Each creak and groan is nature's pledge.

Silent sentinels, watchful and wise,
Reflecting the hues of the bleak skies.
They guard the past, the future too,
In stillness, they hold the world anew.

From mountain peaks to oceans deep,
Their frozen blood in silence sweeps.
Gentle giants, a sight so rare,
In their presence, we breathe the air.

With every thaw, a tale unfolds,
Of warming hearts and ancient molds.
They teach us patience, time's embrace,
Silent glaciers, a lasting grace.

Ethereal Tundra

Endless expanse, white as a dream,
Under the sun, a gleaming beam.
Where shadows dance with the silver light,
A landscape quiet, a wondrous sight.

Whispers of wind through the frozen land,
Each breath a promise, a gentle hand.
Above, the heavens paint skies of blue,
Below, the earth wears a cloak of dew.

Life finds a way in this hushed domain,
Resilient spirits, yet tender and plain.
From mosses green to the wildflower's bloom,
Ethereal beauty in nature's womb.

Stars twinkle brightly in the endless night,
The dance of the auroras, vivid and bright.
In this realm, a harmony sings,
Of solitude's joy and the peace it brings.

As seasons shift and the tundra shifts,
New tales emerge, and the spirit lifts.
Each moment cherished, a fleeting breath,
Ethereal tundra, where magic rests.

Permafrost Dreams

Deep beneath, a world asleep,
Where whispers of winter secrets keep.
Frozen layers seal them tight,
In permafrost, dreams take flight.

Echoes of life in a time gone by,
Trapped in ice, beneath the sky.
Nature's vault, a history's page,
In this frost, we read an age.

Beneath the surface, stories weave,
Of ancient whispers, we believe.
The echoes linger, the silence speaks,
In frozen depths, the heart still seeks.

As seasons change, the top may thaw,
Revealing wonders, shaping awe.
Yet steady lies the frozen seam,
A testament to permafrost dreams.

In autumn's chill and winter's breath,
Life lies dormant, not yet death.
Each flake a keeper of time's embrace,
Permafrost dreams, in a still space.

Shards of Light on Snow-Capped Realms

In the dawn's embrace, snow glimmers bright,
Each crystal a gem, a dazzling sight.
Mountains adorned, a jeweled crown,
Nature's splendor, no hint of frown.

Whispers of wind, they softly call,
Across the valleys, they rise and fall.
Shards of light dance, a fleeting show,
Painting the world where cold winds blow.

In the hushed stillness, all seems right,
Every heart warmed by morning light.
Beneath the sky, vast and so clear,
Peaceful moments we hold so dear.

Frost-kissed branches, a silhouette,
Nature's canvas, a perfect set.
As day unfolds, shadows retreat,
Life awakens, a rhythmic beat.

In awe we stand, these realms we roam,
Shards of light guide us, lead us home.

The Dance of Snowflakes in Dusk's Warmth

As twilight descends, the first flakes fall,
A delicate dance, enchanting all.
Spinning and swirling, a waltz in air,
Nature's magic, a moment rare.

Gentle whispers, they glide with grace,
Each flake unique, in this vast space.
Dusk wears a gown of softest white,
Cradled by shadows, taking flight.

In the stillness, the world holds its breath,
Captured in beauty, a dance of death.
Yet life feels alive in this snowy hymn,
A quiet reminder in twilight dim.

Laughter echoes, children at play,
Snowflakes fall gently, guiding their way.
In every twirl, in every leap,
The magic of dusk, a memory to keep.

As night draws near, the stars appear,
The dance continues, with nothing to fear.
Each flake in the sky, a shimmering spark,
Illuminating dreams that light up the dark.

Quietude of the Frozen Expanse

In the frozen expanse, a silence profound,
A world wrapped in white, untouched ground.
Footsteps muffled, they barely sound,
In this pristine realm, serenity found.

The breath of the earth released in a sigh,
Underneath blankets where secrets lie.
Time stands still, in this tranquil place,
Where nature whispers, revealing grace.

Frozen rivers mirror the skies,
Reflecting dreams that softly arise.
Each distant hill holds stories untold,
In the quietude, the heart turns bold.

Beneath the white veil, life still thrives,
A pulse of the earth in the cold, it survives.
Moments of stillness, a gift in disguise,
In the frozen expanse, our spirits rise.

As twilight deepens, the stars gleam bright,
In the quietude, we find our light.
Wrapped in the peace of this silent shore,
We come alive, longing for more.

Beneath the Luminous Frost

Beneath the luminous frost, dreams ignite,
The world transformed in silvery light.
Each branch a sculpture, every flake shines,
Whispers of beauty, nature's designs.

Night cloaks the land, magic unfolds,
In frozen stillness, a treasure of gold.
Stars twinkle softly, like diamonds arrayed,
Painting the sky where mysteries played.

The moon casts shadows, long and serene,
Illuminating paths where we've always been.
Under this glow, we wander and roam,
In the heart of winter, we find our home.

Footprints in snow tell stories unspoken,
In the chill of the night, hearts remain open.
Embraced by frost, we dance in delight,
Beneath the luminous frost, love takes flight.

As dawn watercolors the sky ever bright,
We hold onto magic that lingers each night.
For in every moment, beneath winter's guise,
The beauty of life in stillness will rise.

Whispering Winds of Winter's Edge

Whispers dance on frosty air,
Silent songs of nature's care.
Trees wear cloaks of purest white,
Stars above, in velvet night.

Footprints left on glistening ground,
Echoes of the past abound.
Breezes weave through branches bare,
In this hush, a gentle prayer.

Chill wraps tight around the heart,
Winter's brush, a work of art.
Moonlight spills on snowflakes' grace,
Time slows down in this embrace.

Each breath forms a fleeting cloud,
Nature's beauty, still and proud.
Whispers linger, soft and low,
Winter's edge, a cherished glow.

Chasing Shadows on Frozen Lakes

Skates carve lines on icy glass,
Children laugh as moments pass.
Shadows stretch beneath the glow,
Chasing dreams when breezes blow.

Reflections dance on frozen sights,
Magical in winter nights.
Laughter echoes, spirits rise,
In this realm, the heart complies.

Beneath the sky of swirling gray,
Hope ignites in joyful play.
Navigating this serene lane,
Chasing shadows, free from pain.

Muffled sounds in winter's grip,
Nature whispers with each slip.
Frosty breaths, a fleeting trail,
Through the woods, a soft exhale.

Skating wild on frozen dreams,
Life, it flows in silver streams.
Merging shadows, hearts align,
In this dance, so pure, divine.

Crystalline Echoes Beneath a Shimmering Veil

Beneath a veil of sparkling light,
Crystalline echoes take to flight.
Nature's gems in smooth display,
Whispers of the night and day.

Each flake falls with soundless grace,
Twinkling in their secret place.
A symphony of frost unspun,
In harmony, all things are one.

Glacial whispers brush the trees,
Carried softly by the breeze.
Every glimmer, every chime,
Feels like a dance with perfect rhyme.

Footprints drawn in snowy art,
Echoes linger, never part.
In this realm of dreams and light,
Life unfurls in pure delight.

Crystalline wonders, silent sound,
In their beauty, hope is found.
Beneath the veil, the heart takes flight,
In winter's embrace, all feels right.

Frost's Embrace on Silent Peaks

Silent peaks in morning's glow,
Frost's embrace, a hush we know.
Veils of white across the height,
Whispers carried in the light.

Mountains wear their crystal crowns,
Majestic in their silent towns.
Every ridge and valley speaks,
Forgotten tales in icy streaks.

Crisp air fills the lungs with peace,
Nature's hold shall never cease.
Moments linger, sweetly freeze,
In this calm where hearts find ease.

Winds entwined with dreams untold,
Frosty air both brave and bold.
Together, we shall climb and soar,
In frost's embrace, life's evermore.

Time stands still, the world expands,
Within these peaks, the heart understands.
Frost's gentle touch, a soothing balm,
In winter's arms, we find our calm.

A Tapestry of Snow and Stars

A blanket of white falls soft and still,
Under a sky where silence shall thrill.
Each flake a whisper, a secret untold,
Dancing in moonlight, bright and bold.

Footprints are lost in the shimmering snow,
Every step forward, a dream in tow.
The stars above glisten, a heavenly guide,
In the tapestry woven, where wonders reside.

Trees dressed in silver, their branches awake,
Holding the night like a fragile keepsake.
The chill in the air, a breath of pure peace,
While nature's soft symphony offers release.

Time seems to pause, as the world turns white,
Crystals of frost catching soft morning light.
In this canvas of magic, calm hearts unfold,
As stories of winter begin to be told.

Together we wander, hearts wrapped in grace,
Finding our solace in this quiet embrace.
A tapestry woven with snowflakes and stars,
Each moment a treasure, no matter how far.

Essence of Frost in the Quietude of Night

In the softest whisper of winter's breath,
Lies the essence of frost, a dance with death.
Crystalline edges trace on the glass,
In shadows that linger, where echoes may pass.

Moonlight spills silver on landscapes serene,
A tranquil reflection of moments unseen.
Every glint of frost tells a tale of the night,
Where beauty and silence blend in pure light.

Branches are laden with delicate lace,
Creating a wonderland, a quiet embrace.
Each crystal of ice holds a fragment of dreams,
In the heart of the night where magic redeems.

The world holds its breath as time drifts away,
Wrapped in the stillness, in twilight's decay.
In the essence of frost, we find our way home,
In the hush of the night, we are never alone.

Glimpses of starlight, a soft shining guide,
Leading us gently through winter's proud tide.
In shadows we gather, our souls intertwine,
In the essence of frost, pure love we define.

Through the Mirror of a Frost-Laden Day

Awakening softly to a frost-laden morn,
The world framed in crystal, anew and reborn.
Each breath hangs like fog, in the chill of the air,
Mirroring whispers of frost everywhere.

Sunlight breaks through like a warm, golden song,
Melting the edges where shadows belong.
The beauty of winter, in glistening hues,
Tells stories of mornings painted in blues.

Fields draped in velvet, a soft winter quilt,
Every corner of nature in elegance built.
Reflections of trees standing tall and proud,
A moment of stillness, where life's not so loud.

Nature's mirror shows faces, both young and old,
In the dance of the frost, their stories unfold.
Through the day's journey, in laughter and cheer,
Every glance of the snow makes the heartbeat clear.

At sunset, a palette of colors displayed,
Reminds us of warmth, though the frost has delayed.
Through the mirror of this frost-laden day,
Lies beauty and wonder, guiding our way.

A Glimpse of Serenity in Sapphire Skies

Amidst the expanse of sapphire skies wide,
Lies a glimpse of serenity, a moment of pride.
Clouds drift like whispers, so soft and so fair,
Painting a canvas with delicate care.

The sun kisses edges of mountains afar,
Bringing a warmth that ignites every star.
In the hush of the evening, where light starts to fade,
A gentle reminder of dreams that we'd made.

Birds rise on wings with a freedom divine,
In rhythms of nature, they deftly entwine.
Each flutter a promise of what lies ahead,
In the tapestry woven where fears gently shed.

Beneath this vast ocean of cobalt and hue,
The heart finds a whisper, a comfort so true.
A glimpse of serenity, in daylight's embrace,
Paints hope in each shadow, each thoughtful trace.

As twilight descends, every star takes its place,
A mosaic of wishes, a celestial grace.
In sapphire skies glowing, we find our way home,
Feeling the love in this vastness we roam.

The Imprint of Time in Crystalline Landscapes

In valleys deep, the shadows lie,
Where ice-kissed stones in silence sigh.
The mountains wear a frosted sheen,
Each peak a tale, both brave and keen.

Whispers of ages carved in frost,
Memories held, and never lost.
Frozen rivers, a ribbon white,
Reflecting dreams in pale moonlight.

Crystalline shards that catch the sun,
Glimmer and sparkle, one by one.
A moment frozen in the air,
Time lingers softly, unaware.

Beneath the stars, the world distills,
The quiet dance of valiant wills.
Each breath of wind, a fleeting chime,
Echoes the imprint of lost time.

In this serene, enchanted space,
Nature's hand has left a trace.
A landscape stitched with history's thread,
Where every step is gently led.

Boundless Stillness Beyond the Hills

Beyond the hills, the silence reigns,
A tranquil hush that softly pains.
The sky unfolds in pastel hues,
A canvas ripe with gentle muse.

The grass lies still, a sea of green,
Embracing peace, a soothing scene.
Each whispering breeze caresses slow,
Filling the heart with quiet glow.

Mountains stand as ancient guards,
Their watchful eyes like timeless cards.
The valleys breathe, the heavens sigh,
Both vast and small, they unify.

In moments shared with endless sky,
The soul can wander free, awry.
Lost in thoughts like drifting sails,
Where stillness wraps and kindness hails.

Timeless beauty graces the land,
With every step, we understand.
The heart seeks solace far and near,
In stillness, we find what is dear.

Frost-Blanketed Echoes of Reverie

Amidst the hush of frosty nights,
The world adorned in silver lights.
Each breath a cloud, each step a dream,
In whispered echoes, soft and keen.

The trees stand tall in icy gowns,
Their branches bear the winter's crowns.
Silent sentinels, still and grand,
Guarding secrets of the land.

As twilight falls, the shadows blend,
A lullaby that night will send.
Frost-blanketed roads, a gentle trace,
Leading us to a sacred space.

Memories twinkle in the air,
A dance of snowflakes, pure and rare.
In reverie, we lose our way,
Drifting softly, night turns to day.

And as the dawn begins to break,
The frosted dreams we softly shake.
In echoes sweet, the heart will find,
A world where time is unconfined.

Windswept Dreams on Luminous Fields

Across the fields where dreams take flight,
The windswept whispers greet the night.
A tapestry of stars unfold,
As stories ancient are retold.

Each blade of grass sways in the breeze,
A symphony composed with ease.
The moon casts silver upon the land,
Guiding footsteps, gentle and grand.

In twilight's glow, the heart can soar,
Chasing shadows to the distant shore.
A luminous path, so radiant, bright,
Awakens hope beneath the night.

The dreams that linger, soft and clear,
Are carried forth, forever near.
Windswept tales of the wild and free,
Embrace the soul with harmony.

Beneath the stars, we dance and sway,
In fields where dreams find their way.
With every breath, the spirit gleams,
Awash in a world of endless dreams.

Candles of Ice in a Timeless Realm

In the quiet glow of night,
Candles flicker, pale and bright.
Whispers dance upon the air,
Ice and dreams entwined with care.

Frozen tears on windowpanes,
Echoes of forgotten gains.
Stars above, a distant call,
In this realm, we rise and fall.

Shadows cast by candlelight,
Painting tales of sweet delight.
Every flame, a story spun,
In the dark, we are as one.

Gliding softly through the frost,
Moments cherished, never lost.
Time stands still, it holds us tight,
In the glow of silver light.

Crystals form on every breath,
Life and beauty dance with death.
Candles flicker, hearts are free,
In this realm, just you and me.

Dim Glimmers on an Endless White Canvas

On the canvas, white and wide,
Glimmers shine, where dreams abide.
Softly painted strokes of light,
Whispers of the winter's night.

Frosted patterns weave and twine,
In the silence, all is fine.
Each glimmer tells a hidden tale,
Of lost journeys, soft and frail.

Footprints tread on snow so deep,
Memories that softly seep.
Underneath the crystal star,
Wonders lingering from afar.

Distant shadows drift and sway,
Holding close the fading day.
Brushstrokes of a life once known,
On this canvas, we have grown.

With each breath, the world renews,
Painting dreams in shades of blues.
Dim glimmers call, a siren's song,
In this silence, we belong.

The Weight of Silence in Winter's Breath

In the stillness, whispers fade,
Frozen echoes, softly laid.
Each sigh a promise, frail yet true,
In winter's breath, we start anew.

Still the trees in cloaks of white,
Guarding secrets of the night.
Every flake a silent word,
In this world, not one is heard.

Time stands still in the cold embrace,
Of a landscape, pure, a sacred space.
The weight of silence holds us tight,
In the heart of winter's night.

Underneath the silver sky,
Hope emerges, does not die.
In the quiet, souls collide,
Finding warmth where love can hide.

So let the world be hushed and bare,
In this moment, hearts laid bare.
The weight we carry, light as air,
In the beauty, truth we share.

Veils of Light on Chilled Horizons

Veils of light on distant hills,
Painting dreams that time fulfills.
Chilled horizons softly gleam,
In the twilight, a tender dream.

Colors blend, a whispered prayer,
In the cold, we feel the air.
Every hue a silent vow,
Joy and peace, we find here now.

As the dusk begins to rise,
Magic weaves across the skies.
Softly do the shadows grow,
In their depths, the secrets flow.

Auroras dance with graceful ease,
Wrapping souls in winter's breeze.
Veils of light, a gentle guide,
On this journey, side by side.

As day bids a tender farewell,
In our hearts, new stories swell.
With each step on chilled terrain,
Veils of light, our love's refrain.

Cold Boundaries

In the grip of winter's breath,
Shadows stretch, like whispers, slow.
Frozen edge, a heart in depth,
Nature's stillness, soft and low.

Boundaries drawn in white and gray,
Each step cautious on the frost.
Beneath the chill, warmth slips away,
Memories linger, but are lost.

Silent trees wear coats of ice,
Branches creak with each cold sigh.
Underneath this stark device,
Life holds on, but dreams can die.

Cloudy skies, a heavy shroud,
Horizon blurred, where shadows creep.
In the silence, winter's crowd,
Holds its secrets, vast and deep.

Yet within this frosty reign,
Hope still stirs beneath the snow.
When the sun returns again,
Cold boundaries begin to glow.

Lunar Frost

Underneath the silver glow,
Fields of frost breathe night alive.
Whispers dance in the cool flow,
Stars twinkle, and shadows thrive.

In this realm of dreams so bright,
Moonlight spills on every crest.
Silhouettes embrace the night,
Lunar frost, an endless quest.

Glassy whispers kiss the ground,
Nature holds its breath in peace.
In the quiet, magic found,
Frozen beauty, night's release.

Crisp air carries tales untold,
Of past seasons winding back.
Frosty patterns, soft and bold,
Mark the paths we often lack.

Beneath the pale and serene glow,
Life awakens, gently spry.
From the frozen depths we grow,
With lunar dreams, we learn to fly.

Veil of Silence

In the hush of morning light,
Whispers fade, untouched by sound.
A shroud of mist, a fragile sight,
Where secrets of the heart are found.

Thoughts drift softly, intertwine,
Wrapped in stillness, pure and thick.
Only shadows, no defined line,
In this silence, time moves quick.

Waves of quiet, calm embrace,
Each heartbeat echoes, soft and slow.
Nature stirs in hidden grace,
Caught within the veils we sow.

Beauty thrums beneath each breath,
Life persists in shadows' play.
In this silence, dance with death,
The dawn will come to light the way.

Underneath the veil so sheer,
Existence hums a timeless tune.
In the silence, truth is near,
Fragments glisten like the moon.

Whispering Hail

Falling gently from the sky,
Whispers turn to silver tears.
Each small drop a fleeting sigh,
Marking pathways through the years.

In the storm, a lullaby,
Nature sings in hurried tones.
Much like dreams that soar and fly,
Caught in feelings, hearts like stones.

Hailstones dance on rooftops high,
Sounding laughter, brittle, sweet.
Nature's voice will never die,
In each collision, lives complete.

Echoes ring through trees and air,
As the world takes on the gray.
Hidden tales in frigid glare,
Whispering of the night and day.

When the storm has hushed its roar,
Quiet reigns, a calm unfolds.
In the silence, hearts restore,
Whispering hail, a tale retold.

Stillness of the North

In the quiet woods so deep,
Nature holds its breath in peace,
Snow blankets all, a gentle sleep,
Time in this stillness seems to cease.

Whispers ride the crisp, cold air,
Footprints vanish without a trace,
Frosted branches stand so bare,
Embraced by winter's soft embrace.

The distant howl of a lone wolf,
Echoes through the frozen pine,
Underneath the ancient elf,
Secrets lost in white, divine.

Stars peek through the velvet night,
Shimmering on the silent ground,
A world transformed by silver light,
In this stillness, peace is found.

Home to dreams that wander free,
Beneath the moon's soft, watchful eye,
North's embrace, a symphony,
Where silence sings and spirits fly.

Dreaming in Winter White

Snowflakes dance on winter's breath,
Glistening like tiny stars,
In their beauty, we find depth,
Each a wish from lands afar.

Blankets of white, a soft cocoon,
Holding secrets, quiet and deep,
Cradled in the night's soft tune,
Nature's promise, sweet and steep.

Children's laughter fills the air,
As they tumble, leap, and slide,
Joy in the season's frosty stare,
In their hearts, the warmth inside.

Fires crackle, a warm embrace,
Hot chocolate warms each hand,
Gathered voices in one place,
Spreading love across the land.

In dreams of winter, we take flight,
Holding magic, fleeting, bright,
In these moments, pure delight,
We find our peace in winter white.

Shrouded in Snow

Whispers in the falling snow,
Nature's hush, a sacred rite,
Every flake an overflow,
Of winter's charm and soft delight.

Trees adorned in crystal dresses,
Silent sentinels they stand,
Each branch holds its cold caresses,
In this serene and quiet land.

Footsteps muffled, echo faint,
As shadows stretch in twilight's glow,
In this moment, none can paint,
The peace we find, so sweet and slow.

Clouds above, a silken cover,
Enveloping the world below,
In this calm, there's always a lover,
In the magic that the snow can show.

Wrap your heart in winter's cloak,
Let your spirit gently flow,
In the stillness, let love soak,
As we are shrouded in pure snow.

Glistening Dreams in Frosted Skies

When dawn breaks with a golden light,
The world awakens, pure and bright,
In frosted skies, dreams take to flight,
Glistening visions of winter's might.

Sunshine kisses the icy peaks,
Painting scenes that nature speaks,
In every crevice, beauty seeks,
Caught in wonder that winter tweaks.

Birds take wing, a graceful dance,
Through sparkling air, they twist and prance,
In every glance, a fleeting chance,
In this moment, we find romance.

With every breath, the chill is sweet,
Frosted whispers, calm, and neat,
In this winter, life is replete,
A canvas where our dreams compete.

Embrace the chill, let the heart soar,
In this beauty, we explore,
Glistening dreams, forevermore,
In the winter's soft, enchanting lore.

Glacial Reflections

In the stillness of the ice,
Whispers dance on frozen seas.
Mirrored thoughts, a silent price,
Time drifts slow in gentle breeze.

Crystals gleam in morning light,
Shattering night with purest hue.
Each shard a spark, a fleeting sight,
Holding secrets, old yet new.

The world above, it seems so near,
Yet deep beneath, all is still.
Water's breath, a sigh sincere,
Echoes linger on the chill.

Beneath the surface, tales untold,
Frozen heartbeats press and pulse.
In every glimmer, stories bold,
Reflecting dreams that time repulses.

In silence loud, the echoes reign,
Frigid beauty haunts the air.
A calming touch, a gentle pain,
Bound to nature's frozen snare.

Polished Silence

The hush descends like morning dew,
A cloak of calm, it wraps the space.
In every breath, the echoes grew,
Soft whispers weave a gentle grace.

Among the trees, the stillness reigns,
Nature holds a quiet ease.
Each leaf, a note in soft refrains,
Rustling secrets on the breeze.

The world moves on, but here it waits,
A moment caught in timeless thread.
Within the pause, the heart elates,
In silence, every word is said.

No sound to break the tender spell,
Just solitude's embrace so fine.
In polished silence, we can dwell,
Revealing truths in every line.

Listening close, one hears the light,
Painting shadows in the day.
In every sigh, a new delight,
Polished silence leads the way.

Celestial Glaze

Stars twinkle high in velvet skies,
Painting dreams in shades of night.
Underneath, the world complies,
Wrapped in the soft, celestial light.

The moon, a guardian so bright,
Watches over every fold.
Casting glimmers, clear and white,
Igniting stories yet untold.

Planets dance in cosmic flow,
A waltz that time cannot confine.
Each shining orb, a tale to show,
In the silence where stars entwine.

Galaxies spin in timeless grace,
Whispering secrets of the vast.
In the night's embrace, we find our place,
A shimmering connection to the past.

As dawn approaches, colors blaze,
Chasing shadows, bringing morn.
Yet in the heart, a soft phase,
The celestial glaze will not be torn.

Frigid Reveries

In winter's grasp, dreams softly sigh,
Snowflakes weave their delicate thread.
A canvas white that clouds the sky,
  Frigid thoughts come gently fed.

Each breath a mist, a vapor's kiss,
  In quiet moments, spirits soar.
Finding warmth in frozen bliss,
  Reveries of what came before.

Forgotten paths beneath the snow,
Where whispers echo through the trees.
In every drift, the tales will flow,
  Frigid reveries bring the freeze.

Silhouettes of life concealed,
In icy realms of nature's hold.
A beauty stark, yet gently revealed,
In winter's heart, stories unfold.

With every chill, the heart beats slow,
  Guided by the frost's embrace.
In frigid dreams, we come to know,
The warmth of memories might replace.

A Starlit Path Amidst the Snowflakes

Beneath the night, the stars do gleam,
A path unfolds, a frozen dream.
Snowflakes dance on whispers mild,
Nature hushes, softly wild.

Footprints traced on crystal white,
Guided by the silver light.
Trees adorned in frosty gowns,
A world transformed, where silence crowns.

In this realm, my heart takes flight,
Cradled in the arms of night.
Whispers linger, time stands still,
A starlit path, my soul to fill.

Each breath a cloud in cold air spun,
Underneath the watching sun.
Magic sparkles, ice like lace,
In winter's warm, embracing grace.

Embrace the calm, let worries cease,
On this path, I find my peace.
A journey sweet, where dreams reside,
On starlit trails, where I confide.

Quiet Melodies in the Frozen Ferns

Whispers dance among the ferns,
Where winter's gentle silence churns.
Each leaf a note in crisp air played,
Nature's song, a sweet cascade.

Footfalls soft on snow-kissed ground,
In this stillness, peace is found.
Cool breaths weave through frozen fronds,
Melodies of nature's bonds.

Patterns etched in white and green,
Serenades, serene and keen.
Softly draped, the world adorned,
In this haven, dreams are born.

Time slows down in this retreat,
Nature's heart, a gentle beat.
Through whispered tunes and frozen grace,
In frozen ferns, I find my place.

Stillness holds, and moments gleam,
In quiet woods, I chase a dream.
Every note, a fleeting spark,
In winter's arms, I leave my mark.

Fragments of Light on Glassy Waters

Reflecting skies of azure blue,
Glassy waters cradle hues.
Fragments of light dance and play,
Nature's canvas on display.

Ripples shimmer with the breeze,
Portraying tales of ancient trees.
Each wave a story, softly spun,
In the glow of the setting sun.

Here, serenity finds its home,
In tranquil depths, where heart can roam.
Moments captured, fleeting bright,
On glassy waters, pure delight.

As shadows stretch and daylight fades,
Echoes linger, softly wades.
A world transformed in liquid grace,
In every ripple, a warm embrace.

Through evening hues, my spirit sails,
On whispered winds and gentle trails.
Light and love in each reflection,
Fragments of joy and connection.

Whispers of the Frozen Thaw

With dawn's embrace, the frost retreats,
Whispers linger in the streets.
Nature sighs a gentle breath,
Awakening from winter's death.

Icicles drop like soft goodbyes,
As warmth returns to earth and skies.
Melodies of thawing streams,
Unfolding in the light of dreams.

In tangled roots and budding trees,
Life stirs softly in the breeze.
Each moment blooms, a fresh sunrise,
In frozen whispers, beauty lies.

A tapestry of melting white,
Beneath the sun's embracing light.
Nature's heart begins to thaw,
In every chorus, life draws near.

The earth awakens, spirits rise,
In harmony, beneath bright skies.
Past the chill, new moments unfold,
Whispers of spring in tales retold.

Glistening Reflections on Quicksilver Peninsulas

The sun dips low, a gleaming light,
Casting shadows, day into night.
Waves whisper softly, a rhythmic song,
On quicksilver shores where dreams belong.

Seagulls dance in a breeze so sweet,
Each echoing call, a heart's pulsing beat.
Footprints washed by the gentle tide,
Memories linger where silence abides.

The sky ignites in hues of gold,
Stories of sailors daring and bold.
Against the horizon, the colors blend,
In nature's embrace, with time to spend.

Beneath the surface, secrets swirl,
Unfurling tales of the ocean's pearl.
Mysterious depths, a hidden lore,
Of lives entwined on the shifting shore.

As twilight fades, the stars emerge,
With each twinkle, our souls converge.
In every reflection, a story remains,
On quicksilver peninsulas' alluring plains.

Snowbound Echoes of Forgotten Tales

Snowflakes fall like whispered dreams,
Covering earth in silvery seams.
Each flake a tale from ages past,
In winter's hold, the die is cast.

Silent woods, a quilt of white,
Shadows deepen with fading light.
The trees stand tall, a ghostly choir,
Singing songs of forgotten fire.

Footprints trace on a winding path,
Leading to realms where memories laugh.
Echoes linger in the crisp, cold air,
Of laughter shared, of love laid bare.

The frost-kissed night brings stories near,
Of a winter's heart, both sharp and dear.
In the stillness, every whisper calls,
As snowbound echoes in twilight sprawls.

As dawn breaks soft with blush and glow,
Forgotten tales begin to flow.
In the arms of winter, we recall,
The warmth of hearts, the magic of all.

The Silence Between Snow and Stars

In the hush of night, a canvas white,
Snow blankets all, concealing light.
Stars twinkle softly, a gentle sigh,
In the silence, dreams dare to fly.

Each flake a wish, a secret shared,
On the breath of night, all is laid bare.
Between snow and stars, we find our way,
Guided by hope, not led astray.

The universe twirls in cosmic grace,
Starlit reflections on winter's face.
Silent whispers float in the air,
As we breathe deep and let down our hair.

In the stillness, we forge anew,
With silver shadows and skies so blue.
In moonlight's dance, we meet the night,
The silence cradles our hearts so tight.

Together we weave through the frosty sphere,
With every heartbeat, find solace here.
Between snow and stars, love shines bright,
In the quiet pause of endless night.

A Cascade of Crystals Under Moonlight

Moonlight spills on a silver stream,
A cascade of crystals, a haunting dream.
Each droplet sparkles, a twinkling kiss,
In the night's embrace, we find our bliss.

The river flows with secrets soft,
Whispers of magic as hearts lift off.
Reflections shimmer in tranquil grace,
A dance of shadows, a fleeting trace.

Glimmers rise like stars in flight,
In crystal cascades, love takes flight.
The air is laced with an icy breath,
A promise woven between life and death.

Beneath the surface, a world untold,
In every ripple, our stories unfold.
Nature's symphony plays through the night,
In the moon's glow, we find our light.

As dawn approaches, the magic wanes,
But memories linger in silvery chains.
A cascade of crystals, forever we'll hold,
The beauty of moments, in hearts like gold.

Breath of Winter Across the Vastness

Whispers of cold in the twilight,
Snowflakes dance in the fading light.
Across the hills, a silent plea,
Nature wrapped in tranquility.

Brittle branches, a crystalline show,
Echoes of silence, soft and slow.
A world transformed, under a cloak,
In winter's breath, we gently spoke.

Footprints mark the way we tread,
In the stillness, thoughts unsaid.
Bitter winds caress the night,
A canvas blank, pure and white.

Stars twinkle in the frozen air,
Beneath their glow, dreams we share.
Embers fade, the fire's glow,
In your arms, warmth still flows.

Crisp shadows under the pale moon,
Time moves slowly, a haunting tune.
Winter's breath, a fleeting kiss,
In silence, we find our bliss.

Reflections of a Chilling Dawn

The horizon blushes, pale and bright,
A chilling dawn, a promised light.
Frosty fields, all aglow,
As nature stirs from the night's low.

Birdsongs echo, crisp and clear,
Each note a whisper, close and near.
Dewdrops glisten on blades of grass,
In this moment, we let time pass.

Clouds drift softly, painted pink,
The world awakes, begins to think.
Breath of frost in the crisp air,
In this beauty, hearts laid bare.

A blanket of white, so pure, so bright,
Lifting spirits, chasing the night.
Reflections dance on every stream,
In the dawn's light, we dare to dream.

As shadows fade, the sun will rise,
Casting warmth across the skies.
In every heartbeat, we resonate,
With the charm of dawn we celebrate.

Boundless White Under Starlit Canopies

A sea of white beneath the night,
Starlit canopies, spirits take flight.
Whispers of snow on the gentle breeze,
Carried softly among the trees.

In this realm of frosted grace,
Time slows down, we find our place.
Moonlight dances on silvered ground,
In quietude, lost souls are found.

Silent echoes, shadows gleam,
Every flake holds a secret dream.
Crystals shimmer under the light,
Hearts entwined in this magic sight.

Beneath the stars, our hopes take wing,
In the stillness, a song we sing.
A tapestry woven with care and love,
Boundless white, blessed from above.

As night unfolds, we dare to feel,
The depth of chilly dreams surreal.
In starlit skies, we find our way,
In this boundless white, forever stay.

A Fragile World of Frosted Dreams

In a fragile world, winter's sigh,
Frosted dreams beneath the sky.
Delicate patterns on windowpanes,
Whispers of beauty in soft refrains.

Snowflakes tumble, twirl, and spin,
Each one unique, where dreams begin.
A gentle hush, a serene embrace,
In winter's dance, we find our place.

Frozen streams, a glassy surface,
Reflect the sky's calm purpose.
In this stillness, we hold our breath,
In the heart of winter, life and death.

Twinkling lights on branches bare,
Frosty nights, love fills the air.
In the silence, secrets bloom,
Within this world, there's no room for gloom.

A tapestry knit from tender spells,
In this fragile charm, our spirit dwells.
Amidst the frost, we find our peace,
In winter's dream, our hearts release.

Crystal Veils

Beneath the moon's soft glow, it weaves,
A tapestry of frost on lacy leaves.
Each sparkling thread, a story told,
In whispers bright, yet fiercely bold.

Like diamonds hung on nature's brow,
The world awakens, silent now.
Nights wrapped in shimmering silk's embrace,
Time stands still in this tranquil place.

Dewdrops cling to branches bare,
A crystal veil drapes everywhere.
The winter's kiss, so cold and clear,
Dances softly, drawing near.

In every corner, magic stirs,
As mystery within the frosty whirs.
With each heartbeat, the night unfolds,
New wonders waiting to be told.

So let us wander, hand in hand,
Through this enchanted, frozen land.
With every step, our spirits soar,
In crystal veils, forevermore.

Shimmering Frost

In dawn's embrace, it glimmers bright,
A world adorned in purest white.
Each flake a spark, a fleeting gift,
As daylight's warmth begins to drift.

Trees stand tall in icy grace,
While sunlight dances on their face.
A shimmering frost, a spellbound sight,
Transforming earth to pure delight.

Footprints left on this crystal stage,
Echo softly like a turning page.
The silence speaks in gentle tones,
Of nature's art, her tranquil homes.

Underneath the frost, life hides,
In stillness where the spirit abides.
The promise of spring, a whispering thought,
In shimmering frost, hope is wrought.

Let us embrace this fleeting chill,
As winter's heart begins to thrill.
With every breath, life's wonders bloom,
Beneath the frost, dispelling gloom.

Winter's Breath

In the hush of winter's breath,
A world transformed by icy wreath.
The air, a crisp and biting thrill,
Wraps the earth in a silver chill.

Clouds drift low, so soft and grey,
While shadows dance at end of day.
Each whispered gust tells tales of old,
In winter's grasp, both fierce and bold.

The rivers freeze, a glassy sheen,
Reflecting skies of pale marine.
Beneath the ice, life holds its sway,
Waiting for a warmer day.

Fires crackle, warmth inside,
While outside, nature's dreams abide.
In every breath, the chill ignites,
As we gather close in winter nights.

Through frosty woods, our footsteps sound,
In silent realms, magic found.
With winter's breath, the world suspends,
A sacred pause where time extends.

Chill in the Air

A chill in the air, so sharp and clear,
Whispers of winter gently draw near.
The sky, a canvas of slate and grey,
As seasons shift and autumn gives way.

Leaves fall softly, a rustling song,
Nature's symphony, both sweet and strong.
The breeze carries scents of woodsmoke fine,
Inviting all to share in its design.

In every corner, life seems to pause,
Animals curled up, a winter's cause.
Frosted windows, patterns aglow,
Reflecting warmth through the ice and snow.

As twilight falls, the stars ignite,
In the chill of the beautiful night.
With cozy fires and laughter shared,
The chill in the air, no longer bared.

So gather close, let spirits soar,
In the embrace of winter's lore.
Through snowflakes dancing, love finds its way,
In the chill of the air, we'll forever stay.

Winter's Lullaby Across Still Waters

Silvery moonlight on the lake,
Whispers of night begin to wake.
Gentle ripples soothe the shore,
Nature's hush, forevermore.

Snowflakes dance on a tender breeze,
Crisp and calm among the trees.
Stars above, a twinkling choir,
Hearts united in winter's fire.

Softly calling to the night,
Dreams take flight in pure delight.
Wrapped in blankets, warm and deep,
Winter's lullaby, we keep.

Frozen breaths on chilly air,
Moments cherished, hearts laid bare.
Hushed reflections glide and slide,
In stillness, we take pride.

As dawn breaks soft across the land,
Nature's canvas, white and grand.
Each gentle wave sings a tune,
Winter's lullaby, afternoon.

Lacework of Frost Against a Midnight Canvas

Under a blanket of endless night,
Silvery frost glimmers just right.
Nature's artistry, pure and bright,
Lacework adorning all in sight.

Stars twinkle like diamonds aglow,
Whispers of winter began to flow.
Each icy branch, a delicate thread,
Painting the darkness where dreams are fed.

Midnight's breath brings a silent chill,
Nature pauses, the world stands still.
With each frostbitten eddy and stream,
We lose ourselves in a shimmering dream.

Velvet skies wrapped tight around,
Secrets of winter's beauty found.
A canvas of frost, bold and grand,
Crafted with care by winter's hand.

In this quiet, magical place,
Time drifts softly, a gentle grace.
The lacework whispers to the trees,
Drifting, twirling on the breeze.

Secrets of the Crystal Dreams

In shadows deep where dreams reside,
Crystal whispers burn inside.
Frosted visions glimmer bright,
Embrace the magic of the night.

Echoes soft of tales untold,
Twilight secrets, bold yet cold.
Glimmers dance on branches bare,
Winter's breath, a chilling air.

Wonders born in frosted gleams,
Awakening our deepest dreams.
Each snowflake tells a story rare,
Nature's sculptures hanging there.

Underneath the starlit dome,
We find a place that feels like home.
Frozen wishes softly gleam,
Embracing secrets of the dream.

In quiet moments, peace we find,
In crystal dreams, hearts intertwined.
Listen close, the night will show,
Secrets only winter knows.

Beyond the Echo of Frosted Whispers

Through the woods where shadows play,
Frosted whispers guide the way.
Silent footsteps on the ground,
In winter's grasp, magic is found.

Beneath the boughs where cold winds sigh,
Echoes drift like birds that fly.
Frosty breath upon the air,
Secrets held with gentle care.

Stars weave through the night's embrace,
Casting glimmers, timeless grace.
Every breath a story spun,
In the night, we become one.

Nature's chorus sings so sweet,
Each heartbeat an echo, a rhythmic beat.
Beyond the frost, the heart can soar,
Discovering what winters store.

In the hush where time stands still,
Let the magic of night fulfill.
Beyond the echo, dreams ignite,
In the beauty of the night.

The Glistening Edge of Daybreak

The sun creeps softly, shy and bold,
Painting the sky with hues of gold.
Whispers of light, they softly play,
Awakening dreams from night's sway.

The dew-kissed grass glimmers anew,
Each blade a jewel in morning's view.
Birds take flight on the gentle breeze,
Chasing the shadows among the trees.

Colors blend in a sweet embrace,
Nature awakes, its heart has a place.
Clouds drift by in a tranquil dance,
While the world stirs, caught in a trance.

A chorus of life fills the air,
Songs of joy both vibrant and rare.
The glistening edge, a fleeting gift,
In the dawn's glow, our spirits lift.

In this moment, all feels so right,
As day breaks free from the frost of night.
Hope springs forth with the sun's soft rays,
Guiding our hearts through endless days.

Where Frost Meets the Fading Light

In twilight's hush, a whisper grows,
Frost melts softly where daylight flows.
Shadows stretch with a hopeful sigh,
As stars peek out in the velvet sky.

Pale remnants of winter cling near,
While warmth encroaches, drawing near.
The earth breathes deep, a softened plea,
As sunlight's glow returns to be.

Branches shimmer with a gentle grace,
Crystals dance in a slow embrace.
Night's curtain falls, a quilt so fine,
Crafted of dreams where lovers pine.

The chill retreats, a lover's kiss,
In the calm of dusk, a tranquil bliss.
Moments linger, suspended in time,
Where frost meets light, so pure, sublime.

In this sacred space, hearts find home,
Bathed in hues where shadows roam.
A symphony plays, soft and bright,
Where frost meets the fading light.

In the Embrace of Frozen Serenity

Beneath the canopy of winter's breath,
Silence blankets the earth in death.
Snowflakes drift in a gentle swirl,
A quiet peace as dreams unfurl.

Icicles dangle from rooftops high,
Like crystals formed in the torrent sky.
A world asleep, so pure, so still,
In the embrace of frozen will.

The moonlight dances on the icy streams,
Reflecting the beauty of slumbered dreams.
Every corner whispers ancient tales,
Where serenity in silence prevails.

In this realm, time softly weaves,
A tapestry of snow-laden eaves.
Hearts find solace, wrapped up tight,
In the embrace of the tranquil night.

Moments linger, untouched, serene,
A quiet hymn, a sweet routine.
In the arms of winter's tender plea,
We find our rest, so wild and free.

Pallor of Dawn on Frostbite

The pale light breaks, a fleeting dream,
Chilling whispers in the morning beam.
Frost clings tightly to each soft breath,
In the stillness, echoes of death.

Shadows shrink in the dawn's soft glow,
While nature softly begins to flow.
Each edge is sharpened by winter's bite,
As day unfolds, claiming the night.

Beneath the frost, life stirs anew,
Emerging from winter, colors unglue.
Yet, in this pause, the world holds tight,
To whispers of cold and lingering night.

In every breath, a gentle ache,
As day awakens with a soft shake.
Pallor of dawn, a canvas bright,
Painting the shadows with hints of light.

Hope flickers in the morning chill,
A promise heard as the world stands still.
In the balance of warmth and frost,
We find the beauty in all that's lost.

Glimmering Chill

The moonlight whispers soft and still,
A breath of frost, a glimmering chill.
Stars twinkle bright, a silver lace,
In the quiet night, dreams interlace.

Trees stand tall, their branches bare,
Crystals dance in the frosty air.
Nature's breath, a pure delight,
Wrapped in the arms of a winter night.

Footsteps crunch on the frozen ground,
In this magic, solace is found.
The world is hushed, with secrets to share,
Amidst the chill, love lingers there.

A flicker of warmth in the cold,
Memories made, stories told.
In glimmering silence, hearts ignite,
Under the stars, in the soft twilight.

Snowflakes swirl in a playful dance,
A moment captured, a fleeting chance.
In the glimmering night, we feel alive,
With every heartbeat, together we thrive.

Echoes of Cold

In the stillness, echoes resound,
The chill of winter blankets the ground.
Whispers of frost in the evening air,
A haunting melody of nature's glare.

Beneath the sky, a canvas of gray,
The world transformed in a frozen ballet.
Each breath a cloud, a moment to seize,
In the echo of cold, we find our peace.

Frostbitten branches hold secrets tight,
While shadows dance in the pale moonlight.
Silence reigns where laughter once flowed,
In echoes of cold, the heart is bestowed.

Glimmers of warmth in the quiet night,
A flickering flame, our guiding light.
Together we stand, hand in hand,
In the echoes of cold, we make our stand.

With every step, we leave our mark,
In the chill of the night, we ignite a spark.
Embracing the frost with every sigh,
Echoes of cold, as time drifts by.

Frostbitten Serenity

In the calm of night, a blanket of white,
Frostbitten serenity wraps the sight.
Snowflakes tumble, a soft embrace,
Nature's palette, a tranquil space.

Whispers of winter in the air,
Each breath a story, each snowflake rare.
The world holds its breath, in silence we stand,
In frostbitten serenity, hand in hand.

Stars above in a velvet sky,
Glimmer brightly as moments fly by.
In every shadow, a hint of gold,
In frostbitten peace, our hearts unfold.

The crunch beneath, a rhythmic sound,
In the stillness, our dreams are found.
Wrapped in warmth, the fire's glow,
Frostbitten serenity starts to flow.

In the gentle hush, we find our way,
Through winter's embrace, come what may.
Together we journey, through chill and cheer,
In frostbitten serenity, we hold dear.

Cascade of Crystals

A cascade of crystals glistens bright,
Reflecting dreams in the pale moonlight.
Snowflakes shimmer, a dazzling sight,
Whirling softly in the still of night.

The earth is clad in a silvery hue,
Nature's wonders, a sparkling view.
In every flake, a story unfolds,
A cascade of crystals, pure as gold.

Through icy branches, the soft winds weave,
Creating wonders that hearts believe.
In this enchanted, wintery scene,
A cascade of crystals, calm and serene.

Footsteps echo on the frozen ground,
In the magic of night, beauty is found.
With every twinkle, our spirits soar,
In the cascade of crystals, we long for more.

As dawn approaches, the glimmers fade,
Yet the memories linger, serenely made.
In the heart of winter, forever bright,
A cascade of crystals, pure delight.

Slumbering Peaks

In silence high, where eagles soar,
The slumbering peaks stand evermore.
Cloaked in white, they guard the skies,
As whispers of the wind arise.

The stars above in quiet grace,
Reveal the night's enchanting face.
Beneath the moon, they seem to dream,
In nature's soft, ethereal gleam.

Time holds still, as shadows play,
Upon the slopes of ice and clay.
Here tales are born from ancient stone,
In valleys deep, where life has grown.

The mountain's heart beats strong and low,
To secrets only few can know.
Beneath their gaze, we find our place,
In harmony, with nature's grace.

Awake we rise, to greet the sun,
In slumber's peace, our souls are spun.
With every step, we forge our way,
Among the peaks where dreams do play.

Fractured Ice

Cracked beneath the winter's weight,
A silent world of frozen fate.
Shards of white in sunlight gleam,
A fractal dance, a winter's dream.

Beneath the surface, life does hide,
In shadows deep where secrets bide.
The echoes of a past long gone,
In icy realms, where hopes have drawn.

Each fault line tells a tale untold,
Of nature's art, both fierce and bold.
The fractures form a canvas wide,
Where time and freeze in silence bide.

Colors swirl in chilly air,
A spectral breath, a frozen flair.
Yet through the cracks, the warmth will seep,
Awakening dreams from frozen sleep.

In every crevice, whispers grow,
Of journeys past in ice and snow.
With each new thaw, the world will change,
Revealing paths that feel so strange.

Unfolding Shards

From fractured rocks, new life begins,
In nature's grasp, where beauty spins.
Each shard of earth with stories clear,
In colors bright, their songs we hear.

The winds of change, they twist and churn,
As vibrant shades in sunlight burn.
Transformation waits in patient grace,
To reveal the heart of every place.

Amidst the chaos, patterns rise,
A tapestry that mesmerizes.
With every turn, new forms take flight,
In shadows cast by waning light.

The world unfolds, a work of art,
A symphony that stirs the heart.
In every shard, a tale resides,
Of moments lived and love that guides.

With open eyes, we seek and find,
The lushness cradled deep inside.
In every crack, a chance to see,
The magic spun from earth and free.

Beyond the Cold

In shadows deep, hope flickers bright,
Beyond the cold, there shines a light.
The frost may bite, but hearts are bold,
In every breath, a warmth unfolds.

Through icy winds, the spirit fights,
To rise again, to reach new heights.
Each challenge faced, a lesson learned,
In fires of faith, our dreams are burned.

The path is steep, yet we ascend,
With every step, the will to mend.
For through the chill, we find our way,
And in the dark, we learn to play.

With arms outstretched, we greet the dawn,
From winter's grasp, our hopes are drawn.
In every star, a promise glows,
That life persists, and love still flows.

Beyond the cold, the blossoms bloom,
In gardens bright, dispelling gloom.
With every breath, we weave our fate,
And in this warmth, we celebrate.

Frosted Vistas

In the hush of winter's grace,
Fields lay still, a white embrace.
Footsteps crunch on crystal ground,
Nature's peace is all around.

Trees wear coats of powdered snow,
Shimmering in soft moon's glow.
Silence reigns, a sacred space,
Whispers of the chilly trace.

Icicles like daggers hang,
In the breeze, the cold winds sang.
A canvas painted pure and bright,
Frosted vistas dazzle night.

Misty breath in starlit air,
Crisp and clean, a frosty flair.
Every branch, a sculptor's art,
Winter's beauty floods the heart.

As dawn breaks with golden hue,
Frosty trails turn wet with dew.
Awake, the world in silent awe,
Nature's magic; winter's law.

Glacial Whispers

Mountains loom with icy breath,
Secrets held in frozen depth.
Gentle murmurs, nature's song,
Echo softly, all night long.

Crystals dance in fleeting light,
Glacial whispers, crisp and bright.
Every turning leaf reflects,
Stories of the frost it protects.

In the shadows, silence glows,
Frozen breath where no one goes.
Tenderly, the world stands still,
Hearts entwined with winter's thrill.

Hushed beneath a silver sky,
Hopeful dreams in snowflakes lie.
Winds carry tales from afar,
In the chill, we find our star.

As night falls, the earth exhales,
Glacial whispers weave their tales.
Quiet echoes, softly spoken,
In these words, the ice is broken.

Chilling Echoes

Beneath the frost, the earth sleeps deep,
In chilling echoes, secrets keep.
The world is wrapped, a cozy shroud,
In whispers low, no sound too loud.

Footprints fade in falling snow,
A silver carpet, soft and slow.
Wind's caress, a gentle sigh,
Through the trees where shadows lie.

Every breath, a cloud of steam,
Capturing winter's fleeting dream.
Voices blend where silence reigns,
Chilling echoes sow their pains.

In the distance, wolves do call,
Nature's pact, a solemn thrall.
Guided by the moon's pale shade,
All is still, as night cascades.

With dawn, the echoes start to fade,
A vibrant world of light displayed.
Chilling echoes, now just a thread,
Weaving warmth where once was dread.

Frozen Dawn

At the break, a world reborn,
In hues of pink, the day is sworn.
Frosty fingers reach for light,
Whispers dance in morning's height.

Glimmers on a silver lake,
Every wave, a moment's wake.
Nature stretches, yawns aloud,
In the sun's embrace, so proud.

Frozen dew begins to melt,
In its warmth, a truth is felt.
As shadows fade and colors play,
The dawn ignites a brand new day.

Birds take flight, a joyful choir,
Hearts ablaze with pure desire.
Winter's shroud, a fleeting guest,
In frozen dawn, we find our rest.

As sun climbs high, the chill subsides,
In golden rays, the warmth abides.
A symphony of life anew,
In frozen dawn, dreams come true.

Beyond the Whisper of Frozen Pines

In silence deep, where shadows creep,
The trees stand tall, in slumber's sweep.
Each breath a chill, the air so still,
Guarding the secrets winter will reveal.

The moonlight dances on crystal ground,
With every step, a hush profound.
Echoes of dreams, in frosty breath,
Whispers of life, in the heart of death.

Footprints trace paths through tangled woods,
Where time holds still, and nature broods.
The nightingale's song, a memory fades,
As dawn breaks through the silent glades.

Icicles shimmer, like jewels of night,
Transforming the world in soft, silver light.
A symphony woven from frost and air,
In the stillness, magic lingers there.

Beyond the whisper, the pines still stand,
Guardians proud, of this frozen land.
With each heartbeat, the world aligns,
In the crisp embrace, beyond the pines.

Frost-Kissed Reveries at the Day's End

As daylight dims, the colors fade,
A tapestry woven, each thread cascades.
Violet hues blend with the deepening blue,
Whispers of twilight, in softest view.

Frost-kissed dreams on windowpanes lie,
Reflecting the stars in the velvet sky.
The chill in the air, a gentle caress,
Wraps the evening in a silken dress.

Cerebral echoes of laughter once bright,
Dance through the dusk, fading from sight.
The crackle of fire brings warmth to the cold,
While stories of old in the shadows unfold.

Moonlight cascades on the blanket of snow,
A path to the heavens, where icy winds blow.
In this calm moment, the night holds its breath,
As we linger in beauty, beyond life and death.

The stars twinkle softly like diamonds aglow,
In a canvas of darkness, they silently show.
Frost-kissed reveries wrap us in dreams,
At day's gentle end, where nothing is as it seems.

The Breath of Winter's Ghost

In the stillness of night, whispers arise,
Breath of winter, beneath starlit skies.
Pale shadows stretch in the moon's soft glow,
Secrets of ages in the cold winds blow.

Branches adorned with a crystalline lace,
Each flake a story, a fleeting trace.
Echoes of laughter fade with the chill,
As warmth slips away, time's longing thrill.

Crickets dim down, their song now a sigh,
As frost wraps the earth, where memories lie.
The ghost of the season dances so near,
In the silence of time, it whispers our fear.

With every breath, the icy air sings,
Carving our thoughts like delicate wings.
A moment suspended, in stillness we float,
In the breath of winter, our dreams gently coat.

When winter departs, and spring starts to glide,
We'll carry those whispers, deep inside.
For the breath of winter, though fleeting, remains,
A haunting reminder of life's many chains.

An Oasis of Cold in a Warm World

In a vibrant realm where the sunlight prevails,
Lies a frozen haven where silence exhales.
A fleeting escape from the tumultuous heat,
An oasis of cold where stillness repeats.

Snowflakes descend on the meadow's green sigh,
Painting each moment beneath the blue sky.
With each crisp breeze, the worries drift far,
In this sanctuary, beneath the North Star.

The trees wear white as their garments of grace,
Shimmering softly, they hold their own space.
In the hush of the night, the world finds its pause,
Embraced by the cold, without any cause.

Here, in this refuge, the heart feels alive,
As the warmth of the sun begins to revive.
In stark contrast, the frosty touch clings,
An oasis of wonders that winter brings.

So let us wander in this frosted embrace,
Where peace flows gently, and time has no place.
In the warmth of our hearts, the chill is a friend,
In an oasis of cold, where silence won't end.

Ethereal Veils in the Glacial Hush

Whispers drift through the frigid air,
Soft as sighs in the twilight fair.
Veils of frost like delicate lace,
Covering the world with a gentle grace.

Moonlight bathes the snow in glow,
Dancing shadows, a silent show.
Trees stand tall in their icy attire,
Embracing the chill, their limbs aspire.

Glimmers of stars in the still night's dome,
Echoes of peace in a frozen home.
Each flake that falls, a whispered tale,
Crafted in beauty, ethereal veil.

Nature holds breath in the glacial hush,
Time slows down in the quiet rush.
Each moment frozen, a jewel bestowed,
In winter's embrace, our spirits flowed.

In the night's cradle, serenity thrives,
Wrapped in wonder, the heart derives.
From silence deep, a world is spun,
In ethereal veils, we are one.

The Serenity of Frozen Shores

Where the ocean meets the frozen land,
Waves whisper secrets, soft and bland.
Icicles glisten like crystal seas,
Nature's harmony in the wintry breeze.

The horizon fades where blue meets white,
In the cold embrace of tranquil night.
Footprints trace tales on the pristine sand,
Marking the journey, hand in hand.

Seabirds glide on the brisk, pure air,
Wings spread wide; freedom laid bare.
In this realm where time moves slow,
The heart finds peace in the frozen flow.

Sunrise ignites the snowy scape,
Colors bloom like a painter's drape.
Each ray a promise, soft and warm,
Amidst the hush, winter's charm.

Serenity reigns on these frozen shores,
As nature whispers, the spirit soars.
In quietude deep, the soul can find,
A gentle refuge, peace entwined.

Twilight's Kiss on Wintry Ferns

Under twilight's soft embrace,
Ferns wear frost, a silver lace.
Whispers of dusk in a chill-kissed sigh,
A dance of shadows as day waves goodbye.

Velvet petals with icy tips,
Frozen dew on nature's lips.
Each breath hangs in the dimming light,
A moment caught, pure delight.

Hues of purple blend with gray,
As twilight ushers the end of day.
Ferns stand proud in their winter coat,
Nature's elegance, every note.

Stars awaken in the evening sky,
Casting dreams as the night draws nigh.
In the hush of gloom, the heart finds peace,
A symphony soft, a sweet release.

Twilight's kiss in the frosty air,
A tender greeting, serene and rare.
In the world draped in shadows deep,
Nature cradles our souls to sleep.

Tranquil Mornings Wrapped in Snow

Soft whispers greet the dawning light,
A blanket of white, pure and bright.
Frosted branches stretch and sway,
In tranquil mornings, peace finds its way.

Silence reigns where shadows fade,
Every footprint's a memory made.
Gentle flurries dance in the breeze,
Wrapping the world in soft decrees.

The sun peeks shyly, golden hue,
Warming the snow, a tender view.
Each crystal sparkles like diamond dust,
In this stillness, we learn to trust.

Breath hangs softly in the chilled air,
A moment of bliss, beyond compare.
Nature unfolds in a pristine art,
As tranquil mornings embrace the heart.

Wrapped in snow, the world feels new,
Each dawn a canvas, each day a clue.
In winter's grasp, our worries cease,
Finding solace in the purest peace.